iPhone 13 Mi

The Most Complete Step by ...p ... ... g ...
New Apple iPhone 13 Mini Hidden Features and Updates
with Tips & Tricks for iOS 15.6

Perry

Hoover

Disclaimer

The information in this book is based on personal experience and anecdotal evidence. Although the author has made every attempt to achieve an accuracy of the information gathered in this book, they make no representation or warranties concerning the accuracy or completeness of the contents of this book. Your circumstances may not be suited to some illustrations in this book.

The author disclaims any liability arising directly or indirectly from the use of this book. Readers are encouraged to seek Medical. Accounting, legal, or professional help when required.

This guide is for informational purposes only, and the author does not accept any responsibilities for any liabilities resulting from the use of this information. While every attempt has been made to verify the information provided here, the author cannot assume any responsibility for errors, inaccuracies or omission.

Printed in the United States of America

Table of Contents

measures 5.4 inches and has a resolution of 1080 by 2340 pixels. Even though iOS 15 is preinstalled on the Apple iPhone 13 Mini, the device is capable of receiving updates to more recent versions of Apple's operating system.

Memory and Functional Capacity

The iOS 15 operating system and 128 gigabytes of built-in storage come standard on the Apple iPhone 13 mini. There is no way to increase the capacity of the iPhone 13 Mini's internal memory, which is just 6 GB. As a result, you will not have any difficulties when using the phone, and you will be able to save an unlimited number of files—including applications, music, movies, images, and more—without having to worry about running out of storage space.

In addition, the Apple smartphone is powered by the Apple A15 Bionic chipset, precisely as was said previously. Because of this, it provides a

The Apple iPhone 13 Mini weighs around 4.97 ounces when fully charged, which is roughly the same as the weight of the majority of the best smartphones that are the same size. This Apple phone has proportions that are about par for the course (5.18 x 2.53 x 0.3 inches).

Screen real state of the iPhone 13 Mini is measured diagonally, from corner to corner, to determine its size. The Apple iPhone 13 Mini has a multi-touch-capable OLED display that

INTRODUCTION

On September 14, 2021, Apple officially introduced the iPhone 13 small mobile device. The display has a size of 5.40 inches, a resolution of 1080 by 2340 pixels, and a pixel density of 476 pixels per inch. The phone comes standard with these specifications (PPI).

A Hexa-core Apple A15 Bionic processor serves as the brains behind the iPhone 13 mini. The mobile device has 6 gigabytes of random access memory (RAM) and 128 gigabytes of built-in storage space. Wireless charging and Apple's own patented kind of rapid charging are both supported on the iPhone 13 mini.

The iPhone 13 Mini is the most recent mobile device to be introduced as part of Apple's iPhone 13 series. This mobile device is very lightweight, and its design is completely captivating. The phone is offered in a variety of color variants, including Midnight, Blue, Pink, Starlight, and Product Red.

This Apple iPhone 13 small is a fantastic smartphone that comes out of the box with support for dual 4G volte and specific camera accelerators such as a depth processor for precise bokeh pictures. Additionally, it has a display that measures only 6.1 inches. These kinds of mobile phones often feature an excellent balance between their responsive performance and their battery life, in addition to the possibility of boosting their picture quality.

CHAPTER ONE

The Key Features of the Apple

iPhone 13 Mini

- iOS 15 upgradable to iOS 15.6 and later
  versions

- Apple A15 Bionic processor

- 6 GB / 128 GB

- 5.40 centimeters (1080 x 2340 pixel)

- 12 + 12 MP, 4032 x 3024 pixel, auto focus, optical image stabilization

- Li-Ion 2438 mAh battery that is not detachable

Design & Display

Apple's smartphone with two SIM card slots has rounded sides, flat edges, and an IP68-rated metal shell. It also supports twin SIM cards. In addition, the phone has a 5.4-inch OLED display with a resolution of 2340 x 1080 pixels, which provides crisp and vibrant graphics for when the user is playing games or viewing movies.

Although the iPhone 13 Mini is equipped with auto focus, an auto focus or optical system uses a sensor, a control system, and a motor to focus on an automatically or manually selected point or area. While the iPhone 13 Mini is equipped with auto focus, an optical system focuses on an automatically or manually selected point or area. The mobile device includes only one front-facing camera for taking selfies, and it has a sensor with a resolution of 12 megapixels and an aperture of f/2.2.

Only a small minority of Android cameras lack an autofocus feature. The optical image stabilization (OIS) on the primary camera of the iPhone 13 Mini helps to reduce the effects of camera shaking. Optical image stabilization is an absolute need for anybody who shoots without the use of a tripod when using a long lens or in low-light settings.

Camera

On the back of the iPhone 13 mini is a dual camera configuration that includes the main camera with a resolution of 12 megapixels and an aperture of f/1.6, as well as a secondary camera with a resolution of 12 megapixels and an aperture of f/2.4. The configuration for the back camera now includes auto focus.

Performance of the iPhone 13 Mini

Since it is equipped with Apple's brand-new A15 Bionic system-on-chip, which has a quad-core central processing unit, the iPhone 13 Mini is an exceptionally powerful tiny phone. When it comes to performance, the phone easily outperforms the very best that Android has to offer, including the very finest gaming phones.

When compared to the A14 Bionic processor from the previous year, even the fastest CPU that can be found in an Android phone that utilizes the Snapdragon 888 has trouble keeping up.

quicker speed and lag-free performance even while accessing numerous programs at the same time, playing intensive graphics games, and surfing the web.

Nano-SIM cards and e-SIM cards can both be used with the iPhone 13 mini, which is a dual-SIM (GSM and GSM) mobile device. The iPhone 13 small has dimensions of 131.50 millimeters in height, 64.20 millimeters in width, and 7.65 millimeters in thickness, and it weighs 141.00 grams.

Starlight, Midnight, Blue, Pink, and (PRODUCT) RED are the colors that were available when it first went on sale. It has been given a grade of IP68, which indicates that it is dust and water-resistant.

Connectivity

The iPhone 13 small comes with several different connectivity choices, including Wi-Fi 802.11 a/b/g/n/ac/Yes, GPS, Bluetooth v5.00, NFC, Lightning, and 3G as well as 4G. The smartphone is equipped with a variety of sensors, such as an accelerometer, an ambient light sensor, a barometer, a gyroscope, a proximity sensor, and a compass or magnetometer.

Additionally compatible with 2G, 3G, and 4G/LTE networks are the Apple iPhone 13 Mini. This mobile device has a built-in GPS. The Global Positioning System (GPS) is a satellite-based navigational aid that can pinpoint an individual's position on the dry surface of the planet regardless of the surrounding atmospheric conditions. A GPS receiver can be found on most modern smartphones.

The Apple iPhone 13 Mini is equipped with Near Field Communication, sometimes known as NFC, capability. Near Field Communication, often known as NFC, is a kind of wireless communication technology that has a short range and makes life easier and more comfortable for people all over the globe by simplifying the process of conducting financial transactions.

Other Features

The use of sensors contributes to an enhanced mobile user experience. The accelerometer is a sensor that monitors the movement of the phone in different directions as well as its orientation. This Apple smartphone already has a proximity sensor built in. This sensor determines how near the phone is to an external item, such as your ear, by measuring the distance between them.

The iPhone 13 Mini is an IP68 dust-resistant and waterproof smartphone that is secure and robust, making it ideal for use in outdoor environments. This smartphone is equipped with technology that allows for rapid charging, which is helpful in situations in which you want immediate power for your gadget.

There is support for wireless charging built into the iPhone 13 Mini. The transmission of energy from one item to another during wireless charging is accomplished by the use of an electromagnetic field and electromagnetic induction.

Battery

The Apple iPhone 13 mini has a Li-Ion battery that cannot be removed, which provides the smartphone with a strong battery backup. The Li-ion battery requires little to no upkeep and provides a high amount of energy while still being lightweight.

iPhone 13 Mini Software

The iPhone 13 Mini makes its debut with iOS 15 (upgradable to iOS 15.6), which has several quite significant changes. It adds new features like as improved alerts, a mode called Focus, enhancements to FaceTime, and changes to a large number of the programs that come preinstalled on the device, such as Notes and Safari. Apple strives to provide a consistent iOS experience across all of its hardware platforms. The iPhone 13 Mini running iOS 15 will have the same experience as the iPhone 12 Mini. This is because some of the older devices are unable to accomplish certain new things owing to hardware constraints.

One of the most well-liked updates that came with iOS 15 was the relocation of the address bar in Safari to the bottom of the screen, making it much simpler to use your phone with only one hand. This was one of the reasons why Apple chose to make this move. There is not a lot to be said about the software experience on the iPhone 13 Mini, other than the fact that it comes with all new camera functions such as Photographic Styles and Cinematic Mode.

However, the most recent version of iOS is 15.6, and it is possible to upgrade it.

CHAPTER TWO

How to set up iPhone 13 mini

After purchasing your new gadget, the following step is to configure it following your preferences.

How to do it:

1. Start the day by turning on your iPhone: To begin, press and hold the power button located on the side of the device until the Apple logo displays, which will then be followed by the Welcome Startup screen. Swipe up to proceed through the game.

2. Select the nation and language that you most identify with. Users who possess an iPhone may now choose between beginning the setup process as if it were a

new device or transferring their data and completing the process. The available options are listed down below.

3. Create an Account as a New Device, and Ignore the Data Transfer Prompts

4. Once you have inserted a SIM card, turned on WiFi, and sign with your Apple ID, you are ready to go.

5. From the drop-down menu, choose the **"Option setup manually"**. Proceed to the next screen, and then choose a connection to a wireless network.

6. To activate your phone, insert a SIM card and follow the on-screen instructions. It's possible that your phone won't start working for a few minutes. & Make good use of the data on your mobile phone.

7. Enable Face ID and set a passcode with a total of six digits. **Note:** If you would rather have a passcode with four digits, you may choose that option from the Passcode alternatives.

8. Type in the passcode in this box.

9. After that, you will be presented with several different setting options.

- To recover your data, you should use an iCloud backup.

- Retrieve lost information from a Mac or PC.

- Make a transfer using your iPhone.

- Transfer Data from an Android Device

10.   Select **"Don't Transfer Apps & Data"** to avoid transferring your apps or data to save time and continue using your iPhone 13 mini.

11.   Now, After inputting your Apple ID login information, set up the various options, such as Siri, and follow the on-screen setup instructions.

How to Make Use of the Automatic Setup Function on the iPhone 13 Mini

1. Start the new iPhone 13 mini, choose a language, and bring the old and new smartphones as close as possible.

2. A pop-up will show on your iPhone 13 mini, asking you to set up the device using your Apple ID. To continue, hit the **"Continue"** button on the pop-up.

3. Select **"Don't Transfer Apps & Data"** from the menu on your iPhone so that you may use your apps without wasting time.

4. Now, After inputting your Apple ID login information, set up the various options, such as Siri, and follow the on-screen setup instructions.

Instructions on how to update an iPhone

13 Mini

It is recommended that you go with the alternative that is both straightforward and secure, which is to let your device handle iPhone updates. You can check to see whether your iPhone is prepared for an automatic update or if you wish to upgrade your new iPhone 13 mini by following these steps:

1. After the Settings app has been launched, choose **General** from the submenu that appears.

2. Tap **Software Update** on the General tab to update the software.

3. On the Software Update screen, touch the option to Automatically Install Updates.

4. Swipe to the right on the Download iOS Updates and Install iOS Updates buttons until they become green. This will enable the iPhone to handle the rest of the process automatically.

5. If both switches are on, your iPhone will automatically download and install software updates while it is locked and charging overnight if both switches are activated.

Note: If you like, you can deactivate the Install iOS Updates option but leave the Download iOS Updates option active on your device. If you follow these instructions, the update will be

downloaded to your phone, where it will remain until you manually install it.

Manual software update on your iPhone 13 mini

You have the option to handle software upgrades manually if you so want or if the phone is unable to do so automatically for any reason. The following are the steps:

1. After the Settings app has been launched, choose **General** from the submenu that appears.

2. Tap **Software Update** on the General tab to update the software. ***Note:*** Your phone will automatically check for available updates and download them if there are any.

3. If there is an update available, choose **Download and Install** from the menu. Note: Before you wait for the update to download to your phone, you must first accept the terms and conditions of the service.

4. When you are ready to complete installing the update, click the **Install button**.

Listed below are some possible solutions if your iPhone will not update:

If your iPhone will not update, either manually or automatically, you may try these troubleshooting procedures to fix the problem.

- Check whether or not your iPhone is compatible with the latest iOS.
- Verify that you have sufficient room for storing items.

The iOS 15 update will need around 3.24 gigabytes of storage space, however, the installation process will require more space than that. In fact, you'll need around 5 gigabytes worth of free space on your phone to download and install the update.

- Launch the **Settings app**, choose **General** from the menu, and then select **iPhone Storage** to see how much free space is currently available on your device. On the iPhone Storage page, the amount of free storage space that you currently have will be shown at the very top.

How to allow backups to be stored in iCloud

You have the option to create a backup of the data that is stored on your iPhone 13 mini. There are three different methods to use cloud storage: on a Mac, a PC, or both (via iTunes).

What are the steps I need to take to back up my iPhone 13 mini to the cloud?

Creating a backup of your iPhone 13 mini via an online storage service is the most time-efficient choice.

To acquire the necessary knowledge to do so, check below:

1. From the home screen of your phone, go to the **Settings menu**.
2. Following that, you will be required to touch your name.
3. After that, choose **iCloud** from the menu.
4. Choose **iCloud Backup** from the choice that drops down.
5. Using this option, you have the choice of either activating Backup Over Cellular or iCloud Backup. The iCloud Backup feature

will perform a backup of your iPhone 13 Mini once per day provided that it is charging, that it is locked, and that it is connected to the internet through Wi-Fi.

6. If you choose to use the **Backup Over Cellular option**, you will be able to back up your iPhone using your cellular network. It's possible that this feature is not supported by your carrier.

7. In the same menu, you will see the option to choose Back Up Now to begin the process of manually backing up the data on your phone.

How to change the name on an iPhone

Your iPhone's name will show in a variety of contexts, including when you use AirDrop to send files to your iPhone when you use the Find My iPhone app, when your iPhone is linked to your Mac, and when you manage it.

It's a good idea to give your iPhone a unique name, both to make it simpler for other people to identify your device and to add some flavor to the experience.

The following are the stages:

1. On your **iPhone 13 mini**, go to the **Settings menu.**
2. Use the drop-down menu to get to **General > About > Name** and choose it.
3. Erase the name that is now shown and enter a new one.
4. Select the **Done option** from the menu.

Follow these procedures to change the names that are associated with your Apple ID:

1. Navigate to the option labeled Settings.
2. Keep your finger on the **"your name"** button.
3. Choose a name for yourself, as well as a phone number and an email address.

4. At this point, at the very top, tap your name to make changes to it.

CHAPTER THREE

About Apple Pay

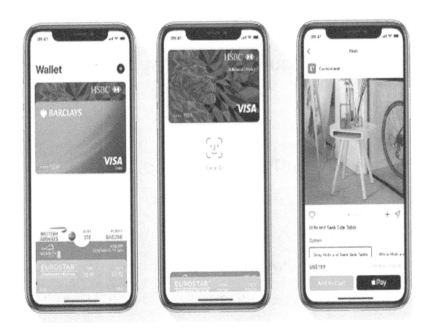

Using Apple Pay on your iPhone 13 Mini is a method of payment that is streamlined, foolproof, and convenient. It is a service provider for digital wallets that was introduced by Apple Inc.

Users can complete financial transactions using their Apple products, such as iPhones, Apple Watches, iPads, and MacBooks. This functionality may be found in subsequent generations of the iPhone, Apple Watch, and iPad Pro (12.9-inch, third generation).

How to configure Apple Pay on iPhone 13 Mini

iPhones have just been released, and one of its newest features is called Apple pay. Additionally, it is obtainable on the iPhone 13 model. If you want to learn how to set up ApplePay on your iPhone, read the steps that are listed below:

The following are the steps to set up Apple Pay on an iPhone 13:

1. Open the **"Utilities"** app on your iPhone 13 Mini and go to the **"Wallet"** section. This will allow you to locate the ApplePay function.

2. At this point, a rundown of how Apple Pay works should appear on the screen for your perusal. After you have finished reading it, click the button that says **"Continue."**

3. When choosing any existing card, pick either **"Debit Card"** or **"Credit Card"** from the drop-down menu. Alternately, you may also put the new card in this spot.

4. At this point, you should see all the cards that are associated with your Apple account on the screen. Choose whatever card you intend to use if you want to use any of them.

5. To add the new card, you can choose the **"Add a Different Card"** option from the drop-down menu.

6. Once you have made your selection, you will be prompted to scan the card to complete the process. After you have scanned the card, please click the **"Continue"** button. If the process of scanning cards does not take place, you have the option of manually adding the data of the card.

7. At this point, enter the security code that corresponds to your card. After that, click the **"Continue"** button.

8. You will be able to see the confirmation message on your iPhone when the card has been successfully added to the device. To proceed, click **"Continue"** once again. (If at any point in the process you

come across the terms and conditions page, give it a single read-through, and then proceed to provide your consent to its terms. You have the option to choose **"Disagree"** if you do not accept Apple's terms and conditions for use of its products and services. On the other hand, you are unable to add the card to your iPhone at this time.

9. When you get to this point, a new page will pop up showing you how to use Apple Pay. After giving it a thorough reading, tap the **"Continue"** button to proceed and return to the **"Wallet"** screen.

When you purchase in-store, in apps, or online, using Apple Pay makes it very handy since it protects all of your cards with security that is at the forefront of the industry.

Using Apple Pay, you don't even need to launch an app to pay for things; all it takes is a simple tap on the Touch ID or Face ID on your device. It is also compatible with a large number of applications that support contactless payments, allowing you to make purchases without having to input your card details or other account information.

Using Apple Pay

If you have satisfied all the requirements outlined in the previous section and are now prepared to use Apple Pay on your iPhone 13 mini, continue with the steps that are outlined below:

1. When you are ready to pay at a store that accepts Apple Pay, you must wait until the cashier tells you that it is time to pay. The presence of light on a credit card terminal often indicates that it is prepared to accept payments.

2. Start by pressing and holding the Side button on the iPhone twice.

3. Position your iPhone 13 mini in the closest feasible proximity to the machine that processes payments.

4. Approve the transaction using your face by looking at the screen of your iPhone while using your Face ID. **Note:** If you're wearing a mask and can't authenticate with your Face ID, you'll need to wait until Apple Pay times out before using it. However, the latest version of iOS allows you to authenticate your Face ID while wearing a mask. After that, choose to Pay with Passcode, and then enter your passcode on your iPhone to finish the transaction.

5. A checkmark indicating that the transaction is complete will appear on the screen of the iPhone, and the payment

terminal will go on to the next step. Your personal identification number (PIN) for your debit card may be requested of you in certain situations.

Steps to take to send money with Apple Pay

- Launch the Messages app on your iPhone 13 mini, begin a new discussion or continue one that you've already started, and then tap the Apple Pay icon to send or receive money.
- Tap the symbol for the App Store if you are having trouble finding it straight away.

Is there a fee that you have to pay every month to use Apple Pay?

Apple Pay does not impose any transaction fees or ongoing service expenses on frequent users of the program. On the other side, Apple receives a transaction fee from the vendors for every purchase.

Which banks and other financial institutions are compatible with Apple Pay?

Apple has global collaborations with major financial institutions and credit card companies like American Express, Bank of America, Discover, and Wells Fargo. The entire list of banks that are partners with Apple Pay may be seen on the Apple website.

Is it risky to make payments using Apple Pay?

Yes. Instead of storing your card information in the Apple Pay app on your smartphone, Apple generates an encrypted identifier for your device and stores it in a secure location on your device. As long as you take reasonable care to protect the private information stored on your iPhone, you have absolutely nothing to worry about.

CHAPTER FOUR

About Apple ID

When using an iPhone, iPad, or Mac operating system, your Apple ID is a crucial component. The Apple ID is required for several programs to operate, including the App Store, iCloud, FaceTime, and iMessage. Additionally, since all of your information, emails, and more are kept on your Apple ID, your Apple ID password is just as important as your ATM PIN.

If your Apple ID password is compromised, you may face serious issues that you may never have to face in your life. This will instantly change or modify your iCloud password.

When setting a new Apple ID password, keep these requirements in mind before changing the current one.

- A minimum of eight characters, an uppercase letter, a number, and a lowercase letter must be included in the Apple ID password.
- Do not use your Apple ID or a previous password, and do not separate your passcode with spaces.

There is no better device than an iPhone to use if you need to update your Apple ID password right now. You may modify the Apple ID password in just a few simple steps.

1. Go to the **"Settings"** app.
2. Tap Your Name.
3. Choose **"Password & Security"**.
4. Select **"Change Password."**
5. Next, you must enter your Apple ID's current password before entering the new one.
6. Finally, choose **"Change Password" or "Change"**.

CHAPTER FIVE

iCloud KeyChain

iCloud Keychain is Apple's password manager for Macs, iPhones, and iPads. It is meant to keep your passwords, credit card information, Wi-Fi logins, and a lot of other vital data secure while also making it much simpler for you to set and remember complicated passcodes.

What does iCloud Keychain do?

You have undoubtedly noticed that iCloud Keychain asks you whether you would want to store a newly entered password in Safari for use on all of your devices whenever you input a new password in Safari.

If you are using iOS 7.0.3 or later, as well as OS X Mavericks 10.9 or later, iCloud Keychain will safely store the following things in the cloud for you: When you have all of these things encrypted in iCloud Keychain, you will be able to access them safely from any Apple device as long as you are signed in with your Apple ID.

- Login information and passwords for the Safari website
- Specifics about credit card numbers
- Information about Wi-Fi network
- Make sure that your Messages, Calendar, Contacts, and Emails are synchronized across all of your devices.
- Protect, get access to, and use the logins and passwords for all of your online accounts, including LinkedIn, Twitter, and others.

How exactly does Apple's iCloud Keychain function?

Every device has to have the iCloud Keychain service turned on. Since information stored by the service can only be accessed by devices that have been enabled for it, you will have to manually input your passwords and any other relevant credentials on any devices that you use.

Where can I find the instructions for using iCloud Keychain in Safari?

When signing up for a new website or service, you will be prompted to input your information into the appropriate areas located on the website's registration page. iCloud will automatically fill up this information with things like your name and phone number, among other things. You will also be required to generate a password by filling in the password box with your new password and the password confirmation field with your new password again.

If you want to use an iCloud-provided password, you will see a little object appear when you press your cursor in the first of these boxes. Also, if you want to use it, tap the item. In fact, your iCloud Keychain should save your password for subsequent use, regardless of whether you choose to use your password or one that is provided by iCloud.

How to add the information for credit card to the iCloud Keychain

You also have the option to upload the information of your credit card to iCloud Keychain. You have the option of following the instructions that appear on the screen to complete this action automatically as and when they do so, or you may input this information manually as follows:

- On a Mac, go to the **Preferences menu** and choose the **AutoFill option**. Find the Credit Cards item, and then press the **Edit button**. You can add new cards as well as remove existing ones when you go on to the next screen. Tap **Done**.

- On an iOS device, go to **Settings > Safari > Autofill**. You can restrict what credit card information is stored, as well as activate or disable the Autofill feature for user names and passwords, under this section. By selecting **Saved Credit Cards**, you will be able to modify or remove the information that has been saved for your saved credit cards. Tap Done.

How to locate website passwords that are stored in iCloud Keychain

There may be instances when you wish to manually verify the information associated with your user name and/or password. You can accomplish this with the assistance of iCloud Keychain, and if you want to, you can even copy and paste the relevant information into other applications. It is quite simple to accomplish:

- To save passwords on a Mac, go to **Safari > Preferences > Passwords**. You are going to be prompted to enter a password. On the next screen, you will see a list of your websites, together with the user names and passwords for those websites. This list may be searched. You can copy and paste them by holding down the **Control button.**

- On an iOS device, go to the Settings menu, choose the **Accounts & Passwords option**, and then touch the **App & Website Passwords option**. After authenticating yourself with TouchID, FaceID, or a passcode, you will be granted access to a list of all the website passwords that you make use of, which can then be searched.

How to turn on/off the iCloud Keychain on my device

Activating or deactivating iCloud Keychain on your device can be done as follows:

- On a Mac, go to the **System Preferences menu**, choose **iCloud**, and then check or uncheck the Keychain box. You will be required to enter your Apple ID and then follow the instructions that appear on the screen.

- On iOS, go to **Settings > Apple ID > iCloud > Keychain**, and turn the switch on (or off). Once again, you will be required to enter your Apple ID and follow a set of instructions that are shown on-screen.

If you wish to activate iCloud Keychain on more than one device, you must repeat these instructions on each of those devices.

What exactly takes place when a new device is added to the iCloud Keychain?

When you enable a new device, an unusual thing happens: all of your other enabled devices will get a notice asking them to approve the new device so that it may join your chain.

You need to manually provide your approval for any new addition that comes from one of your already registered devices. This is a positive development since it indicates that you should generally anticipate receiving a similar warning if someone attempts to put a device into your chain that you do not own. If you get such a request, you have the option to decline it.

In some circumstances, you may not have access to any of the devices you already own. In such a situation, you will be required to use your iCloud Security Code or do anything that requires the SMS phone number that is linked with your iCloud/Apple ID account.

When you initially set up iCloud Keychain, a new iCloud Security Code is generated for your account.

Is Apple's iCloud Keychain a secure option?

The vast majority of consumers are unable to quickly determine whether or not password management solutions provided by third-party suppliers can be trusted. This is not the situation with iCloud Keychain, which was released by a developer who had the resources necessary to respond rapidly if a security flaw is discovered.

Security researchers may on occasion discover possible vulnerabilities, which Apple will often patch very quickly. Keeping the software on your device up to date is the most effective method for preventing unauthorized access to your iCloud Keychain.

Technically speaking, iCloud Keychain offers a very high level of security including:

- The 256-bit Advanced Encryption Standard (AES) is used to encrypt both passwords and credit card details stored in keychains (Advanced Encryption Standard).

- Data is secured using an exclusive (device) key and your device passcode, both of which are known only to you. This ensures that no one else can access your information.

- The use of two different authentication methods is strongly suggested.

Apple also has a policy regarding customers' privacy. When you register for a new online service, for example, iCloud Keychain will both recommend and remember very complicated passcodes for you. This feature is available in situations when such passcodes may be necessary. Because of this, it is much simpler to adhere to recommended security procedures, such as changing your password for each service you use.

What other features does iCloud Keychain have?

You can also generate and keep private notes in your iCloud Keychain while using a Mac. Accessing these kinds of notes requires not only their password but also the password you use to log in to your account, making them exceptionally safe places to save sensitive information like software licenses.

- Launch the Keychain program on your Mac, go to the **"Secure Notes"** menu, and then click the **"Plus"** button to create a new encrypted note. After writing the letter and giving it a name, press the **Add button**. You will need the password that you chose to access that message in the future.

CHAPTER SIX

About Siri

Siri is a digital assistant built into iOS that enables users to operate their iPhones by speaking commands to them. It functions like Amazon's Alexa and enables you to do any action on your smartphone.

You can use it, for instance, to search for music on the internet, surf the internet, answer phone calls, and do a great deal of other things.

The steps:

1. Open the **Settings app**.
2. At this point, go to **Siri & Search** and choose it.
3. After that, pick the option labeled **"Press Side Button for Siri."**
4. To confirm, choose the **Enable Siri option**.
5. To activate or disable Siri on the lock screen, you will need to make sure that the Allow Siri When the Locked option is selected.

And that is all. You can start a conversation with Siri at any time by depressing and holding the Side button until the Siri symbol appears at the bottom of the screen.

Change the Voice of Siri on Your iPhone 13 Mini

1. Open the **Settings app**.
2. Once you've located it, pick **Siri & Search** by clicking on it.
3. Select **Siri Voice**.

Take note that the voice genders that are offered might differ from nation to country and region to area. To switch the language, go to the Siri & Search screen and pick **Language** from the menu.

What Siri Hears When You Speak to Her on Your iPhone 13 Mini

1. You can ask Siri to make a phone call, obtain directions, discover a contact, set reminders and meetings, search the web, identify any music, and do a wide variety of other tasks. You may also ask Siri amusing

questions like "What can you do for me?" and she will show you an example of what Siri can do for you on your smartphone. This can be done by asking Siri a question like "What can you do for me?"

2. In addition, Siri can interpret words and phrases for you. Therefore, you can speak a sentence in a language other than English, such as Chinese or Italian, and Siri will translate it for you into the language of your choice.

3. After that, you will see that an audio orb at the bottom of the screen is moving, which shows that Siri is paying attention to what you are saying and processing it. After that, you will be presented with a conversation with Siri; choose the icon of Siri to continue having a conversation with it.

The Step-by-Step Guide to Getting Siri to Recognize You on the iPhone 13 Mini

To make your interactions with Siri more tailored to your preferences, you will need to ensure that Siri knows and understands you extremely well. To do this, pick **My information from the Siri** Search panel, then go to and select your Contact from there. You are now able to utilize the information at your disposal to ask inquiries such as "How do I go home?" and "What nice eateries are near me?"

Instructions on How to Make Use of Siri Within Apps on the iPhone 13 Mini

Siri is helpful in that it can provide recommendations for shortcuts both on the lock screen and inside applications, and these ideas are determined by how you use the apps.

Suppose you use the same app each morning when you wake up. Siri will save this information and begin offering that app on the lock screen each morning so that it can be easily accessed.

- Go to the **Siri & Search screen**, scroll down until you find the app you want, and then tap the **toggle switch** that you want to use to turn on or off Siri Recommendations in that app or on the Lock Screen. Now you can activate or disable Siri Suggestions on the Lock Screen or in-app suggestions.

The Step-by-Step Guide to Reading Siri Messages on Your iPhone 13 Mini

If you are unable to access your iPhone, you may have Siri read any incoming messages to you directly on your device by using your AirPods. To do that, follow the instructions outlined below.

1. First, go to the settings on your smartphone.

2. Pick the **Notifications menu option.**

3. Choose to **Have Siri Read Out Loud Your Recent Messages.**

4. The last step is to flip the option labeled **"Announce Messages with Siri."**

Note that this functionality is only supported by the AirPods 2 and the Powerbeats Pro and that in order to use it, both of those headphones must first be linked to your iPhone. Siri even allows you to respond to texts by just speaking to her.

5. Select the **Send Replies Without Confirmation setting** to enable Siri to send messages without first reading them to you for confirmation before doing so.

How to Use Siri on an iPhone 13 Mini by Typing Instead of Talking

1. The first thing you need to do is go to **Settings > Accessibility > Siri**.
2. Activate the **"Type to Siri"** feature.
3. At this point, you can make a request, summon Siri, and then use the keyboard and the text box to ask Siri a question or ask Siri to do an action on your behalf.

How Come Siri Doesn't Work on My New iPhone 13 Mini?

It is essential to have an understanding of the factors that are contributing to Siri's malfunctioning to proceed with the implementation of the remedies. In this manner, you will be better equipped in the future to deal with difficulties of this kind. It may be quite upsetting to lose access to Siri's services, particularly if you depend on her for your day-to-day activities.

However, there is something that we need to be aware of, and that is the fact that much like other elements of iOS, Siri is susceptible to small crashes, bugs, and other mistakes that may occur inside the system.

The following are some of the possible reasons why Siri is not functioning:

- Keeping the screen of your iPhone 13 Mini turned down
- Securing the back cover of your iPhone 13 case
- iPhone is in the mode that saves battery life
- Airpods and microphone with a muffled sound
- Incorrect configurations are currently in place
- Unreliable connection to the internet

- Incompatible iOS device (iPhone 6 or earlier)
- The language that is not formatted correctly

The problem with Siri not functioning properly on your iPhone 13 Mini might be attributed to a number of underlying factors, including those listed above. After gaining an understanding of them, you will be able to proceed with putting the relevant solutions against the same issues into effect.

Fixing Siri When It's Not Working on Your iPhone 13 Mini

People who rely heavily on Siri to do their day-to-day activities may find it very difficult to function if Siri is not operating properly, as was discussed previously. However, because you are now familiar with the reasons why Siri does not function properly on iPhone 13 Mini, we can, at last, proceed with addressing the problem's solutions.

To address this problem, the following are some of the most important potential solutions:

1. Force your iPhone to restart

Your phone will provide you with fast relief from any issue that you are now dealing with if you just restart it. This is the first step toward a simple solution. We recommend that if you haven't restarted your phone in quite some time, you make it a practice to do so at least once a week. This is especially important if you haven't restarted your phone in quite some time. By doing so, you can protect your phone from crashing as well as other issues that could interfere with the normal operation of your device.

2. Make sure that "Hey Siri" and any other relevant settings are turned on

Some of your device's settings may be changed without your knowledge if you do an update on it. Because of this, there is a significant possibility that the settings and configurations will be altered, which will result in issues inside the system.

The vast majority of consumers have complained that Siri cannot be opened on their iPhone 13 Mini immediately after the installation of iOS 15 on their devices. In this particular scenario, you may verify and fix the problem by confirming that the options that are detailed below are turned on.

- Go to the Settings menu on your iPhone 13 Mini.
- Open Siri and do your search.
- Confirm that the aforementioned options are active in this section.

- 'Listen for "Hey Siri. "Siri can be accessed using the side button. Simply give Siri when it is locked.

- If these settings are not already active, you may activate them by toggling the switches that correspond to them.

- After you have finished enabling the required options, restart your iPhone and check to see whether the problem is still present.

3. Set Restrictions for Siri and Manage Them

If you have recently upgraded your smartphone, it may sometimes automatically activate the limitations feature on your iPhone 13 Mini, even if you haven't changed any settings. And if you don't have permission to use Siri on your device, you won't be able to use it. To correct this and to better control Siri's limits,

- Go to the Settings menu on your iPhone 13 Mini.

- Tap **Screen Time**

- Navigate to **Restrictions** on **Content and Privacy**.

- Enable **Content Restrictions and Privacy Setting.**

- Navigate to the menu and pick the **Allowed Apps option**.

- Ensure that Siri and Dictation are not disabled by ensuring that they are not switched off.

- To activate Siri and Dictation, just switch them on if they are turned off.

4. Manage Siri Responses

It should come as no surprise that Siri will not react audibly if the volume on your iPhone is muted. A situation similar to this one might arise if you have inadvertently turned off the Siri replies option on your iPhone 13 Mini. If you want to be certain, it is highly recommended that you verify and control Siri's replies on your iPhone 13 by following the procedures that are presented.

- Go to the Settings menu on your iPhone 13 Mini.
- Open **Siri** and do your search.
- Select **Siri Responses**
- Modify the method by which Siri reacts.
- Using the options that are shown to you, pick either Always, Only when **"Hey Siri"** is said, or When Silent Mode Is Off.

5. Turn off the mode that uses less power

For those who are unaware, the Power saving mode that is available on Android is identical to the Low Power Mode that is available on iOS. When you convert your iOS device to Low Power Mode, the mode will instantly terminate any applications or services that were previously operating in the background.

However, one of the most significant effects of this is that Siri will no longer function. If you have already activated the low power mode, you may turn it off by following the instructions indicated below.

- Go to the Settings menu on your iPhone 13 Mini.
- Go to the **Battery menu**.
- Make sure the toggle next to Low Power Mode is OFF

6. Make Sure Your Microphone Is Working

If Siri is unable to understand what you are telling her to do, she won't be able to carry things out. Because Siri is Apple's voice assistant, it primarily processes the spoken instructions that are given to it by its users. If you notice that Siri is not working despite your giving her several instructions, it is highly recommended that you check to see whether or not your microphone is functioning properly.

Siri needs free access to your microphone to perform its functions effectively. Nevertheless, dust, dirt, and water damage may sometimes cause the microphone to get clogged, which prevents the orders from being sent properly.

- Launch any app that enables you to use the Siri and Dictation features to determine whether or not your microphone is functioning properly. Give your instruction by speaking it into the microphone. If you still do not notice any movement in response to the instruction, this indicates that the sound coming from your microphone is either too muffled or not functioning properly.

7. Using Siri, disconnect either your AirPods or any other device

Siri can't work if it is linked to more than one device at the same time, much as with WiFi. You will need to unplug both your Airpods and any other devices that use Siri to get Siri to operate perfectly on a single device. To do this, you will need to turn off the Bluetooth functionality on all the linked devices, except for your iPhone.

This is because Bluetooth is the primary method of communication used by these gadgets. And the gadget that is the only one that will answer your instruction is the one that can hear your request the most clearly. As a result, except for your iPhone 13 Mini, turn off the Bluetooth on every other device that is linked to Siri.

8. Double-check your connection to the internet

Even though voice assistants make our lives simpler, they are still reliant on an internet connection to do all the tasks you ask of them online. Therefore, even a little change in the Internet Connection has the potential to cause Siri's functionality to completely cease. If you notice that Siri on your iPhone 13 Mini is not functioning properly, you should check your internet connection as soon as possible.

If you are currently connected to a Wi-Fi network, you should verify the signal strength. If you discover that the signal strength is low, you should make plans to improve it and restore your Internet connection to get Siri back up and running as soon as possible.

9. Make Sure You Have the Most Recent iOS Update

Apple Developers, just like Android Developers, tend to provide periodic updates for all of Apple's devices. These updates often include bug fixes and take care of any problems that have been reported by users. However, given that you are experiencing issues, the issue most likely stems from the fact that the software you are using is out of the current. To verify whether the most recent iOS update is installed

- Go to the **Settings menu** on your iPhone Mini.
- Go to **General.**
- Go to the **Software Update menu**.
- If there is an available update, choose to install it.
- To finish, click the **Install Now button.**
- After the update has been installed, restart your device.

CHAPTER SEVEN

Contacts

Add contacts to your iPhone using the Contacts app by following these steps:

1. From the home screen of your device, choose the symbol that resembles an address book and has silhouettes of a man and a woman that are grayed out. This is the icon for the **Contacts app**. Launching the Phone app, which is represented by a green symbol and a white phone, and then touching the Contacts icon that is located on the bottom toolbar is another option.

2. To add a new contact, you can do so by tapping the **Plus icon**, which is located in the upper right-hand corner of your screen.

3. Enter the first and last name of the contact, along with any additional information that may be relevant, such as their phone number, email address, postal address, birthday, website URL, and so on. You have to enter information into at least one of these fields before you can save the contact. You can also upload a picture by selecting the **"Add photo"** option located in the upper left corner of the screen.

4. When you are through editing the contact, click the **"Done"** button located in the upper right-hand corner of the screen. This will save the contact.

How to use an iPhone's text messaging feature to add contacts

This is how it is done:

1. Begin sending a text message to the individual whose contact information you wish to add to your phone.

2. Tap their phone number, which is located at the very top of the screen.

3. In the menu that appears directly below the phone number, choose the **"info"** option by tapping on it.

4. On the page that opens up displaying the details, touch the arrow that is located to the right of the field that displays the phone number. Please take note that doing so will bring up a completely blank contact screen.

5. Select **"Create New Contact"** and input the person's first and last name in the appropriate fields.

6. When you are finished adding the contact, touch the **"Done"** button.

How to import contacts from your most recent call logs onto your iPhone 13 mini

You can bring in contacts by using any of these methods:

1. Launch the Phone app and locate the icon that looks like a white phone on a green background. This is the Recents icon, and it's located in the bottom toolbar of the Phone app.

2. On the Recents screen, locate the phone number you want to add as a contact and tap the information option that is to the right of the number.

3. Once the blank contact page has opened, choose **"Add New Contact"** from the menu.

4. Enter the name of the contact exactly as you would want it to appear on your phone, as well as any other information that may be relevant, such as the URL of the contact's website, their email address, etc.

5. After you have finished adding the contact, click the **"Done"** button.

How to block and unblock a number

The following is a guide that will walk you through the process of unblocking a number on your iPhone, allowing the contact to once again call, text, or FaceTime you:

1. From the menu titled Settings, choose the Phone option. On the device you are using

that does not have the Phone app installed, go to **Settings > FaceTime**.

2. From the drop-down box, choose the option to **Block Contacts**.

3. Move your finger from the right side of the number to the left side of the number in the Blocked Contacts list, and then tap the **Unblock button**.

How to Remove Blocked Messages

If you have blocked someone in Messages so that they are unable to reach you through text message, you may unblock their number in the settings for Messages so that they can start sending you messages again.

1. Navigate to the **Settings menu** and choose **Messages** from the submenu that appears.

2. Go to the bottom of the list and click the **"Blocked Contacts"** button.

3. Swipe from the right side of the screen to the left side of the number that you want to unblock, and then tap the **Unblock button**.

Callers can be unblocked once they are added to your contacts list:

- If the blocked number is associated with one of the people in your Contacts list, you need to unblock it from that person's listing. Find an entry for the individual in the app called **Contacts.** It needs to have a tap done on it.

- Once you have done so, click the **Unblock this Caller button** that is located at the bottom of the person's contact information.

Using Contacts App Icon on the Home Screen of an iPhone

When you initially set up your iPhone, the main Home screen will include a few icons that are pre-installed by the manufacturer. However, since there is not enough room on that screen for all the preinstalled applications, the remaining icons have been moved to a secondary Home screen, which can be accessed by swiping left from the primary Home screen.

On your iPhone, it may be difficult to locate some of the applications that you need the most.

Whether it's a default app that isn't located on the primary Home screen or a third-party app that you just installed from the App Store, you will likely want to rearrange the current layout of your icons. This is because there is a possibility that you will want to access a default app that isn't located on the primary Home screen.

You may relocate the Contacts icon since it's a significant symbol. This rapidly opens the contact list that you have stored on your iPhone, enabling you to identify contacts so that you may call them, send them a text message, begin a FaceTime conversation, and do a variety of other actions with them.

Your iPhone's Contacts icon can be moved to the Home screen by going to the second Home screen, opening the **Extras folder**, tapping and holding on the **Contacts icon**, selecting **Edit Home Screen** from the menu that appears, dragging the icon to the location you want it to appear on the Home screen, and finally tapping the Done button when you are finished.

How to Add an Icon to Your iPhone's Home Screen Representing Your Contacts

1. On the first screen that says Home, swipe left.

2. Navigate to and open the **Extras folder**.

3. To access your contacts, tap and hold the **Contacts icon**.

4. Choose the option to **Edit the Home Screen**.

5. Place the **Contacts icon** on the Home screen by dragging it there.

6. Tap **Done**.

Delete numerous contacts from your iPhone at the same time

Whether you've moved on from a job or a relationship or just don't need the number of your old plumber anymore, it's simple to erase contacts from your iPhone. You can even take the further step of blocking a contact after you have deleted them from your phone's address book, preventing them from calling or texting you in the future.

The steps necessary to remove contacts on an iPhone 13 Mini

There are three different approaches to erasing contacts from an iPhone.

Delete individual contacts

1. Launch the **Contacts app** on your iPhone, or open the green Phone app and choose

the Contacts tab located at the bottom of the screen.

2. Once you have located the contact whose information you no longer desire, touch on their name.

3. On the details page for the contact, locate the top-right corner and choose **Edit**.

4. After scrolling down to the very bottom of the screen, choose the option to delete the contact by clicking the red text that says **"Delete Contact."**

5. When the pop-up window appears, choose the **Delete Contact option**.

Delete several contacts all at once

To complete this task, you will need access to a computer. Be aware, however, that to store contacts in advance, you will first need to configure your iCloud account.

1. Visit the website for iCloud and sign in using the credentials associated with your iCloud account. There is a possibility that you may need to input a code that was provided to your iPhone.

2. Navigate to the page titled **Contacts**.

3. Locate the contacts you no longer need and make a selection of all of them at once. Whether you are working on a Mac or a PC will determine the method that you use to do this task.

- To erase contacts from a Mac, hold down the **Command key** while clicking on each contact you wish to remove.

- To erase contacts from a PC, hold down the **Control key** while clicking on each contact you wish to remove.

4. When you have all of them chosen, click the gear icon in the bottom left corner, and then click the **Delete button**.

5. You will be prompted to verify that you do wish to remove the contacts from your phone. Click **Delete**.

CHAPTER EIGHT

Using Siri for FaceTime call

Are you interested in learning how to make a call using FaceTime with Siri? It shouldn't come as a surprise that you can use Siri to start programs and control your music library. Additionally, although the majority of people are familiar with using Siri to conduct voice calls, it is also possible to utilize Siri to make FaceTime calls.

Using Siri to make calls over FaceTime can be done as follows:

1. Say "**Hey Siri, FaceTime [contact's name]**" after you have Siri switched on.

2. While maintaining pressure on the side button, you can also say **"FaceTime,"** then

the name of the person you want to contact, and then end the conversation.

3. If you mention a name that is connected to many contacts, Siri will ask you to clarify which contact you are referring to when you say that name.

4. Choose the most relevant person to contact.

5. Your FaceTime call will start by itself when you are connected.

How to combine many contacts into one

Since you already possess an iPhone, employing iCloud to manage your contacts should be a simple process for you. Nevertheless, errors are possible, and it may seem that you have a significant number of duplicate contacts on the list of those stored on your phone. You're quite right, the process of locating and removing each item one at a time is tedious and time-consuming.

Since you keep repeating the same contacts [Different name but the same number, Merge contacts that have the same name but different phone number], it is not simple to discover or short duplicate contacts on an iPhone without using any apps if you have a large contact list. This is because you can only shorten the list by merging contacts that have the same name but a different phone number.

The Step-by-Step Guide to Locating and Deleting Duplicate Contacts on an iPhone 13 Mini

1. Locate the **Cleaner app** on the App Store and download it.

2. Launch the **Cleaner app** and create a login by following the on-screen instructions that appear.

3. After you have agreed to the contact access requests, the program that cleans should immediately begin searching through your contacts.

4. Navigate to the tab labeled **"Merge,"** and then choose **"Show Possible Merges"** from the menu that appears.

5. To expand the duplicate contacts, choose the **"Duplicates"** tab in the first section.

6. Tap the information button that is located next to the contact's name.

7. Swipe to the left to avoid merging a contact that you do not want to be merged or deleted as a duplicate. If you come across a contact that you do not want to be merged or removed as a duplicate.

8. After you have selected all the contacts that are duplicates or that need to be merged, tap the **Merge button** at the bottom of the screen.

How to transmit files using Apple's

AirDrop service

AirDrop is a technology that makes it quick and simple to transfer data between iOS devices. It is especially helpful because it is a genuine device-to-device transfer that works even if neither device has an internet connection; nevertheless, for it to function, Wi-Fi and Bluetooth need to be enabled.

Any file that has been shared using Apple software by clicking the share symbol may be sent with AirDrop. Included in this category are a user's photographs, movies, iWork projects, notes, contacts, links, and instructions, as well as their location data. Data may also be sent between devices via AirDrop by using third-party programs. AirDrop is a feature introduced in iOS 15 for mobile devices. It is only capable of transferring files between other mobile devices and not between mobile devices and personal computers.

- To activate **Control Center** and enable **Airdrop**, swipe up from the bottom of the screen in the direction of the arrow. Verify at the very top of the control panel that the Wi-Fi and Bluetooth settings are both set to the **"on"** position.

- When you choose **AirDrop** from the menu that appears, you will be able to choose between Off, Contacts Only, and Everyone. If you choose **"Everyone,"** you will be able to share files with anybody, including those who do not have internet access or an iCloud account.

- If you choose **Contacts Only**, you will be prompted to sign in to iCloud, so you will need to ensure that you have access to the internet. After successfully signing into iCloud, the only people with whom you will be able to exchange and receive files are those who are listed in your contacts. You can make changes to this setting whenever you want using Control Center.

- Even if you choose **Everyone** as your sharing option, you could be prompted to enter your iCloud password at some point. If, on the other hand, you pick **Cancel**, you will be able to share with anybody.

- **Collaborate on Documents or Data:** To get started, you need to use a program that supports sharing. A few instances of this are Safari, Photos, Maps, Notes, Pages, Keynote, Numbers, iPhoto, iMovie, GarageBand, Photo Booth, and Contacts. Pick the files that you wish other people to have access to. You may, for instance, bring up a location or instructions using

Maps. Pick a card to send to a contact from the list. Use the **Select button** located beneath the Photos section to choose one or more still images or movies. After making your selection of the file you want to share, you will need to tap the icon labeled Share. If you are within range of another device that is using AirDrop and it is turned on, the sharing menu of that device will display a circular icon to indicate that AirDrop may be used. Tap the symbol of the device you want to send to make your selection.

- A sound alert will also be played on the device. You can make adjustments to this sound by going to **Settings > Sounds > AirDrop**. When large media files, such as movies, are being transmitted, a progress indicator in the shape of a circle will show. A confirmation message is shown on the device that is receiving the large file once it has successfully been sent. On the device that is doing the sending, there will also be a confirmation that the file was transmitted without any problems.

Quick file and data sharing is made possible for customers who do not want to make use of iCloud, which is another benefit of the AirDrop application. You can still share individual files with programs that do not support iCloud sharing, even if you already use iCloud. The ability to send data and instructions between devices when in the field, away from Wi-Fi and cell towers, is another benefit of this technology.

CHAPTER NINE

How to set up an emergency

medical ID

Both Medical ID and SOS are features that might save your life in an emergency. Both of these features aren't very eye-catching or often used, which is why it's simple to forget to set up a Medical ID or, in the case of SOS, to be unsure how to use it in an emergency. Having them in place and being familiar with how they function, on the other hand, is of great use.

Users who have Medical ID installed on their devices can preserve vital health information as well as emergency contact information on the Lock screen, where it can be accessed by first responders. When an emergency call is received, your Medical ID can be promptly sent to the appropriate first responders using iOS 15.6.

When it comes to SOS, the activation of the emergency feature can be done in one of two different ways.

How to set up the Medical ID on iPhone or make changes to it

1. Ensure that you are running iOS 15 or later so that you can have access to all the features.
2. Launch the application known as **Health**.
3. Navigate through the brand-new welcome splash screen, which will enable you to configure or update your medical ID and activate the brand-new capability of sharing during emergency phone calls.
4. When you're finished, press **Done**.
5. Click the **Review Medical ID Access button** at the very top of the Health app once you

have completed the process of updating or setting up your health profile, and then proceed with the steps outlined in the prompts that appear.

Remember, too, that you may add more than one person to function as a contact in case of emergency, up to a total of twenty-four. After you have done making changes to your Medical ID profile, you will be able to check your sharing choices. You will find the option to activate the new **"Share Medical ID Information During an Emergency Call"** function located in this section.

To adjust these settings at any time in the future, touch your profile picture located in the top right corner, pick **Medical ID**, then select **Edit**, and then scroll to the bottom of the screen.

Steps to take to modify the SOS settings on iPhone Mini

There are three different ways to activate the SOS feature on your iPhone to get in touch with emergency services. In the most current version of iOS, two of the features that provide a higher level of automation have been set to be enabled by default.

By simultaneously pressing and holding the **Side button** and any of the **volume buttons** on a more recent iPhone, users may initiate a countdown to five seconds. This is what people mean when they talk about an **"Auto Call."**

The second way, known as the **Call with Side Button**, involves rapidly pressing the Side button (or the sleep/wake button), depending on the device. On the screen that allows you to turn the device off, the third choice is the SOS slider.

Changing these settings may be done as follows:

1. Navigate to the option labeled **Settings**.
2. Swipe down and then hit the **SOS button** in the emergency menu.
3. Toggle the settings off and on to choose which SOS features you would want to take use of.

How to download the Apple TV app onto your iPhone 13 Mini

Using the Apple TV app, you can view Apple TV+ original programs and movies, in addition to other shows, movies, sports, and live news programming. You may also add channels to your Apple TV, such as Paramount+ and Showtime, watch movies and television shows that are available via streaming services and cable providers, and purchase or rent movies and episodes.

Using the Apple TV app, which is accessible on your iPhone, iPad 13 mini, Apple TV, and other smart TVs and streaming devices, you can watch on your iPhone, iPad, iPod touch, Mac, Apple TV, and other compatible smart TVs and streaming devices.

It is important to keep in mind that the Apple TV app, as well as its features and services (including Apple TV+, Apple TV channels, sports, news, and compatible apps), are not accessible in every country or region.

Get channels by subscribing to Apple TV

If you subscribe to an Apple TV channel (such as Paramount+ or Showtime), you will have the option to watch an ad-free film on demand or download it to enjoy it when you are not connected to the internet. If you make use of the Family Sharing feature, you will be able to share your membership with up to five other members of your family at no additional cost.

1. First, choose the **Watch Now option** from the drop-down menu. Next, go to the **Channels row** and scroll down until you discover a station that you want to watch.

2. Select the subscription option by tapping on it, then read the details about the free trial and paid subscriptions (if applicable), and finally, follow the instructions that appear on the screen.

You will need to link your cable or satellite subscription after installing the Apple TV app. Through the use of a single sign-on, you will have fast access to all the compatible video programs that come with your subscription package.

1. From the Settings menu, choose the **TV Provider option**.

2. Log in with your provider credentials after choosing your TV provider.

3. If your TV provider isn't listed, you will need to sign in via the app itself if you want to use it.

App for connecting apps to the Apple TV

The Apple TV app will recommend new content to you, such as the next episode of a series you've been watching on another app, or the next episode of a different series entirely.

1. Select **Watch Now** from the menu, then go to **Streaming Apps** to examine the content that is offered.

Perry Hoover

2. Tap an app to connect it, and then proceed with the instructions that appear on the screen.

Take control of your connected apps and subscriptions, as well as your viewing history

1. Click the **Watch Now button**, then click your **profile picture** in the top right corner of the screen.

2. Make your choice from one of the following available options:

- **Connected Applications:** Streaming applications that are supported can be connected or unplugged depending on the user's preference. The Apple TV app notifies you of any linked apps on any of your devices to which you have previously used your Apple ID to log in.

104

- Modify or terminate a subscription by tapping the subscription's name in the **"Manage Subscriptions"** section.
- Clear **Play History** allows you to delete all the watching history stored on your Apple devices.

CHAPTER TEN

Camera App

How to capture burst photos

The iPhone 13 mini's burst mode allows the user to take many images with a single click, or it can be set to take 10 shots automatically after 3, or 10 seconds.

How to capture images in "burst mode"

1. Launch the Camera app on your iOS device, in this case, an iPhone 13 mini.
2. Using your camera's default settings, snap a photo of the scene you wish to record.
3. On the iPhone 13 mini, the Burst mode can be accessed by swiftly pressing and swiping to the left.

4. Out of all the photos, iOS will choose the one that it considers to be the most impressive. If you do not like the options that it recommends, you are free to choose your own.

5. After you have completed your burst capture, choose the thumbnail located in the bottom-left corner of the screen.

6. Choose the **Burst mode** stack that you wish to see.

7. To continue, click the **Select button**.

8. Tap the checkbox next to each photo that you want to keep by using the left mouse button.

9. A gray dot will show below the thumbnail scrubber for the photos that have the best focus and composition.

10. When you've determined what information you want to keep, press the **Done button**.

11. Pick the option to **Retain Everything** if you want to retain all the photographs in

the stack, or choose the option to Keep Only (number) Favorites to remove the other pictures.

12.   The selected photos are now stored individually in your Camera Roll after being ungrouped.

Follow the instructions below to disable the Burst mode on that device:

Disable Burst Mode

1. Open Camera.

2. At this point, locate the **Off button** on the bottom strip of the screen. Tapping this button will switch off the camera timer, which will stop the continuous shooting mode. Take note that this indicates that you can snap many photos with only one click of the shutter button on the camera.

How to switch the camera on the back of your iPhone to the camera on the front of the device

1. Launch the Camera app on your iPhone 13 mini.
2. By touching the Flip camera button, you can switch between the camera that faces forward for FaceTime and the camera that faces backward.
3. Press the **Shutter button** to begin either taking a photo or recording a video.

Create a panorama with your iPhone 13 mini by following these steps:

1. Launch the Camera app on your iPhone 13 mini.
2. To access the Pano mode, swipe to the left twice.

3. If you want to change the direction in which the capture is done, click the arrow button.

4. Press the **shutter button** to snap a photo using the panoramic setting.

5. Tilt or pan your iPhone to get the most comprehensive picture possible of your location and surroundings. Make every effort to ensure that the point of the arrow remains aligned with the yellow advice. Note that the app will give you a warning if you're moving either too swiftly or too slowly.

6. To finish creating the panorama, click the shutter button a single more time.

Take into consideration that the Camera app does not yet allow complete 360-degree panoramas. Keep in mind that you may take a single picture that encompasses all 240 degrees. If you don't want to, there's no need you use all 240 degrees of rotation.

How to make use of the live photo filters available on the iPhone Camera

The steps:

1. Launch the Photos app on your iPhone 13 mini.
2. On an iPhone 13 mini, slide up from above the shutter button or press the arrow at the top of the screen to access the camera roll.
3. Click the button that looks like three concentric circles stacked one on top of the other.
4. Select the filter that you want to apply to the image.
5. Press the shutter button to take a photo with the filter that you have selected applied.

Steps to activate the flash on your camera

1. Launch the Camera app on your iPhone 13 mini.
2. To enable or disable Flash, hit the toggle in the upper right corner.
3. Determine whether you want it to be on Auto, On, or Off, and make your selection accordingly. On an iPhone 13 mini, you can access the Auto, On, or Off settings by touching the arrow located at the top of the screen.

Note: Be aware that if you have the Flash setting on your iPhone 13 mini toggled to On or Automatic, Night Mode will not activate since the flash will be utilized instead. Keep this in mind.

How to film a Cinematic Video

Within Apple's brand-new Cinematic Mode, the **"rack focus"** way of focusing is combined with the Dolby Vision HDR format. Because rack focus creates an impression of depth of field by concentrating the lens's attention on the subject of the shot while blurring the background, the lens may make a seamless transition from one subject to another.

When another subject enters the frame or you manually center the camera on a new topic, Cinematic Mode will automatically adjust the focus point and blur the background.

How to use the Cinematic Mode while taking pictures using the Camera app

Another video style that can be accessed via the Camera app on your iPhone 13 mini is called the Cinematic Option. This is the route that you can take to get there.

1. Launch the Camera app on your iPhone 13 mini.

2. Use your finger to scroll through the menu until you locate the **Cinematic Mode option**.

3. Align the viewfinder so that the subject you want to take is in the center of the frame and the focus point, and then push the **Record button** to start taking pictures.

4. Bring another person or object into the scene and position them at a different distance; at this point, the iPhone 13 mini should automatically refocus and lock onto the new target. You also have the option of manually moving the focus to a different location.

5. When you are done, you can stop the recording by tapping the Record button a second time.

After the shoot, what are the many ways to alter the movie in Cinematic Mode?

The ability to alter the video and manually change the focus point is by far the most stunning aspect of the Cinematic Mode. The procedure is as follows.

1. Launch the Photos app on your iPhone 13 mini.
2. Using the search function, find the movie that you want to use and choose it.
3. To edit, choose the **pencil icon** in the upper right corner.
4. Use your finger to scroll through the clip reel until you find the area that you want to change, and then click it.
5. Tapping a different part of the clip will allow you to manually shift the focus point. A symbol denoting manual tracking will now

be shown in the top left corner of the screen.

6. Below the clip reel, a yellow line with dots appears; this line indicates the amount of time that the manually specified focus point will be watched.

7. You are free to remove the manually monitored focus point at this time.

8. When you are satisfied with the modifications, touch the **Done button**.

CHAPTER ELEVEN

How to record your screen

It can be very useful to record the screen of your Apple iPhone 13 mini in a video with sound and save it as a video file. This can be done to show a friend how to perform certain tasks within an Apple iPhone 13 mini, and the video can then be sent to the friend or uploaded to a platform such as YouTube or a social network.

To generate this recording on your Apple iPhone 13 mini, follow these steps:

1. The first and most important step is to check if the screen recording feature on our iPhone 13 mini is turned on. We can confirm

this by heading to the Settings menu, which is represented by a gear icon on the primary screen of your Apple iPhone 13 mini.

2. We scroll to the bottom of the left-hand menu until we reach the **"Control Center" section**, and then we click on the **"Customize controls"** option.

3. If we have all the screen recording control switched on, it will be shown in the first list under the **"Include"** area on our iPhone 13 mini. We can rearrange the items by tapping on the three horizontal lines that are located to the right of the control and dragging them either up or down. We also have the option to erase the control by hitting the button on the left that is colored red.

4. If the active control is not visible, scroll down until you reach the **"More Controls"** section; if it is there, click the **green "+" button** to add it. After we have finished with this operation, we will be able to leave the settings on the Apple iPhone 13 mini.

5. If you want to record a video on your Apple iPhone 13 mini without using the microphone, press the recording icon; a three-second countdown will begin, and then the recording will begin; a red line will appear at the top of the screen, along with the word **"Recording,"** indicating that everything on the screen is being recorded.

6. If you want to record a video using the microphone instead of the iPhone 13 mini's sound (for example, to explain the operation of an app to a friend or to record a message while recording the video from

119

the screen of the Apple iPhone 13 mini), press and hold the shutter button, then press on the microphone to activate or deactivate it, and then press on **"Start recording."** This will allow you to record a video using the microphone instead of the iPhone 13 mini's sound. After a countdown that lasts three seconds, the recording will start playing.

7. To stop recording, open the **Control Center** and press the button labeled **"Stop Recording."** Alternatively, you can open the status bar at the top of the screen, click on the red line, and then press the **"Stop"** button.

8. A notification has been shown at the top of your Apple iPhone 13's little screen informing you that the screen recording video has been stored in the **"Photos"** folder (formerly known as the Camera Roll). ***Note:***

To see and share the video, open the Photos app on your Apple iPhone 13 mini and search for the video clip that was made when the screen was in its ultimate position.

How to screenshot successfully

The process of capturing screenshots on an iPhone 13 mini is noticeably simpler than it is on any other iPhone model. This is even though there are several compatible applications for Apple devices that enable users to capture **"screenshots."**

The procedure is, for the most part, the same under iOS 15 as it was in previous versions:

1. To turn the device off, hold down both the **Power and Volume Down buttons** at the same time.

2. In only a few seconds, there will be a flash that indicates that the screen has been captured.

3. To capture a video of your screen, you must simultaneously press the buttons labeled **Power and Volume Up** on your device.

How to capture images

On your iPhone 13 mini, the camera app allows you to relive those unforgettable moments in the form of photographs, which is perfect for when you want to share them with others. Taking pictures gives allows you to make memories of events that have happened in the past as well as events that you want to remember in the future.

To do this, you will first be required to unlock your smartphone. Note that you should only do this step if your smartphone is locked; otherwise, go on to the home screen of your device.

After you have brought up your Home Screen, go for the camera app, and then change it to whatever shooting mode you choose (it could be set on portrait or normal mode). After that, you need to press and hold the shutter button for a few seconds so that your shot may be taken.

How to use the portrait mode

A camera option is known as **"portrait mode"** enables the user to focus on the principal subject of the photograph while blurring the background. There is no difference in functionality between this and a DSLR camera.

The following are examples of iPhone devices that support the portrait mode feature:

- The iPhone 7 Plus

- Apple iPhone 8 Plus
- The iPhone X
- Apple iPhone XR
- The iPhone Xs and the iPhone Xs Max (iPhone Xs and Xs Max)
- iPhone 11, iPhone 11 Pro, and iPhone 11 Pro Max are all included.
- The iPhone SE
- Apple iPhone 12 small, Apple iPhone 12, Apple iPhone 12 Pro, and Apple iPhone 12 Pro Max
- iPhone 13 models

How to Take Pictures on Your iPhone

using the Portrait Mode

1. From the Camera menu, choose the **Take Portrait option**. You also have the option to launch the Camera app and choose the **PORTRAIT mode**.

2. Ensure that you are between two and eight feet away from the subject of the photo. If there are any instructions shown on-screen, such as **"going further away,"** you should adhere to them.

3. When everything is in its proper location, the name of the effect will become yellow; for example, **"Natural Light" or "Depth Effect."** Please take note that the blurring of the background will also be evident in real-time.

4. To take a picture, you may either press the button labeled **"Shutter"** or the buttons labeled **"Volume Up" or "Volume Down."**

Note that even if you click the picture after failing to follow the directions shown on-screen and the effect name does not change yellow, the name will not turn yellow even if you click the image. In this particular situation, the photo will have a regular appearance and will not have any background blur effects applied to it.

How to Use Different Lighting Effects on Your iPhone Portrait

You can snap a photo using the Portrait mode of your camera, and then use the Portrait Lighting effect to edit the image. You can also click while using these effects.

1. Launch the **Camera app** on your device, and from the mode drop-down option, choose **Portrait.**

2. Swipe the **Natural Light button** in the viewfinder to choose a **Portrait Lighting effect** and then press the **shutter button**. It achieves this effect by blurring the background while maintaining a sharp focus on the subject's face.

126

3. Make sure to pay attention to the on-screen instructions. ***Note:*** Ensure that the **"Portrait Lighting"** effect's name is changed to **"yellow"** before continuing.

The Step-by-Step Guide to Taking a Selfie in Portrait Mode

The front-facing camera in iPhone X and subsequent models, including the iPhone 13 mini, enables users to capture portrait-style selfies. The process is the same as when taking pictures using the Portrait mode.

1. From the Camera menu, choose the option to **Take Portrait Selfie**. Another option is to open the Camera app and then switch to the Portrait shooting mode

before switching to the front-facing camera.

2. Be sure to follow the instructions that are shown on the screen. It would be helpful if the name of the effect was underlined in yellow.

3. Reduce pressing the button on the camera's shutter. You could also use the volume button on the iPhone, or if the EarPods are connected to the device, you could use them.

How to remove the portrait mode effect that was applied to my photos

Photos taken in portrait mode may be turned into regular photos with none of the background blurring being lost in the process.

To do this, follow the steps:

1. Select **Photos** from the app's main menu, and then select **Albums** from the bottom menu.

2. From the menu of available media types, **pick Portraits**, and then choose a photo to edit.

3. Go to the **Edit menu.**

4. Tap the word **"Portrait"** that is highlighted in yellow.

5. There will be an instantaneous elimination of any blur. Tap the **Done button** to save the image.

CHAPTER TWELVE

How to switch between apps

It is possible to move between programs quickly and easily without having to quit the one you are now using. Using the App Switcher, which is a multitasking view, is one way that you might achieve this goal.

- On the iPhone 13 mini, you can access the **App Switcher** by sliding up from the edge of the display, stopping for a minute, and then sliding up again. This will list your programs in the sequence in which they were most recently accessed, with a screenshot of each application shown alongside the list.

- To access further content, swipe from right to left, then touch any of the screenshots to be taken to the appropriate application.

To dismiss an application that is currently running, swipe up on the screenshot. By swiping up with the same movement, you can close many programs all at once, even if you have more than one finger on your device.

How to exit applications with the back button

With the iPhone 13 mini, there is still a possibility that issues could arise, and you can end up with an application that isn't performing as it should be. When this occurs, it is best to force-close (or force-quit) the troublesome application rather than wait for it to fix itself, which may never happen.

You can forcibly shut an application by using the App Switcher

Likely, you are already acquainted with the process of forcefully stopping programs if you have an iPhone 13 model, including the iPhone 13 mini, since the technique is the same for all of these devices.

- Launching the app switcher is the first thing you need to do to close a running application when you're using Face ID for the very first time. Move your finger up from below the screen of your iPhone, then hold it there for a second before letting go; do this until the app cards appear. Make sure you give yourself a moment to catch your breath before you start swiping to go back to the home screen.

- You can forcibly shut an app by swiping up on its app card when the app switcher is open. To do this, slide sideways until you find the app you want to quit, then slide sideways again. You are free to follow the same steps with any other application that you decide you no longer want. Simply swipe up from the bottom of the screen, and you will be sent back to the home screen.

To restate this, follow the steps below:

1. Move your finger up from below the screen of your iPhone 13 mini, pause for a second, and then release your finger when the app cards show.

2. Swipe to the right or left on the cards to find the app you wish to use.

3. Swipe up from the bottom of the app's card to force the app to close. Note that

this works in either portrait or landscape mode; however, you can only open the app switcher in landscape mode if the app you are using at the moment supports landscape views. Also, note that this option works in either portrait or landscape mode. You also have the option to close several programs all at once. To shut the visible cards, you need just put one finger on each card, then swipe your finger up and away at the same moment. You may cancel as many as four different programs at the same time if your fingers are fast enough.

When it is appropriate to forcibly exit an application and when it is not

It is reasonable to presume that programs that have been opened and are now displayed on your app switcher are using processing power, memory, and battery life on your device. Memory and battery allocation, in addition to background activity management, are all tasks that are handled by the operating system on your iPhone, which in this case is iOS 15.

The recently used applications are simply put into a dormant state when accessed via the app switcher. This means that they are not actively running and making use of any of your iPhone's valuable resources, like its RAM and CPU. Your iPhone devotes all of its processing power to whatever it is currently doing, whether that be displaying the home screen or running an application; however, a portion of that processing power may be allotted to recently closed programs that were terminated in the last five minutes or fewer.

When you exit an app and go back to the app switcher in iOS 14, the software saves a snapshot of the app's current state. When you reopen the application, it will be much easier to recall this information. When you force-close an app on iOS 15, the snapshot is deleted, and the app has to regenerate it when it is reopened. This requires more battery power than if you had just kept the program open in the app switcher.

In a nutshell, you should only use the **"force quit"** feature on your iPhone to close apps if they are acting erratically, have become unresponsive or frozen, or are malfunctioning in some other way. If you believe that one of your apps is causing your iPhone to run more slowly than usual, you have the option to force-quit that program; however, if you are unsure which app is the culprit, it is often simpler to just restart or force-restart the device.

Making Memojis

You can send animated messages in iMessage that look like you by using a feature called Memojis, which is similar to Animoji but uses your device's Face ID instead. To begin going, just carry out the following procedures:

1. On your iPhone mini, launch **Messages** by logging in with Face ID. Please take note that this applies to the iPhone X and all subsequent models.

2. Start a discussion with a person and then press the button with three faces on it.

3. After that, on the left side of the screen, tap the three dots, and then choose **New Memoji**. Note that you will be allowed to modify your face attributes, including your skin tone, hairstyle, and facial features. There are now a variety of different options accessible, including cosmetics, teeth, facial piercings, and more.

4. To send a short video message as your Memoji, press and hold the red recording

button until the message appears on the screen. Simply touching the keyboard once will allow you to add a Memoji or Animoji to a conversation in the form of a sticker. You now have the option of using your Memoji as your photo in the Contacts app.

How to adjust the level of brightness on the screen

Now, using the Control Center in this manner will get the job done. Here's how:

1. Make sure the screen on your iPhone is switched on by checking its status.

2. Swipe down from the top-right corner of your screen to access the next screen.

3. When you reach this stage, a grid of buttons will appear before you. There you will discover the Control Center that you've been looking for.

4. The brightness slider may be found on the right side of the screen. Swiping in either direction across it will allow you to use it.

5. To make more precise adjustments to your input, press and hold the brightness slider.

6. Swipe up or down to increase or decrease the brightness of the display. **Note:** Additionally, do not forget to look at the bottom of the screen to do this. You can also enable additional display options from that menu.

7. To return to your home screen, touch any area of the screen that is not the Control Center.

How to Adjust the Level of Brightness on the iPhone 13 Mini Using the Settings Application

The brightness of your iPhone may also be adjusted using the Settings app, which is available on all iOS devices. This is the proper way to accomplish things.

1. Launch the Settings app on the iPhone 13 mini.

2. Scroll down the page until you reach the bottom of the page. Following that, choose the **'Display & Brightness** option.

3. A slider for adjusting the level of brightness will now display. It is possible to shift it either to the left or to the right.

4. Move the slider to the left to lessen the amount of light that is shown on your screen.

5. To make the display brighter, move the brightness slider to the right.

Remember that the brightness of the display on your iPhone is automatically controlled by sensors that detect the amount of ambient light (by default). There are several circumstances in which this feature might prevent your phone from achieving its highest possible level of brightness. In a scenario like this one, our recommendation is to disable the capability.

CHAPTER THIRTEEN

How to set up Family Sharing

Through the use of the Family Sharing feature, not only are you able to make all of your iTunes and App Store purchases available to your relatives, but you can also make it such that younger family members need your approval before purchasing anything. After that, you could receive a request, and you can decide whether to accept it or not straight from your iPhone 13 mini. The following is a rundown of everything you need before getting began.

Everything You Need to Know About Family Sharing

When using Family Sharing, you can include up to six members of your immediate family. To function, every smartphone has to be running iOS 8 or later (up to iOS 15.6 and later versions if any). As soon as you are linked to one another, you will have instant access to each other's purchases. You will be able to see and download these items anytime you choose, just as you would from your account.

Remember that any purchases made after that point will be charged to the iTunes account of the person who organized the family gathering, so keep that in mind. The only exception to this rule is if the customer's iTunes account has enough store credit to cover the cost of the purchase. In this scenario, the individual account store credit will always be used before any other kind of credit.

An Overview of the Features of Family Sharing

- You can instantly share any purchased content, including music, movies, books, television shows, and more.
- You can rapidly share images with other members of your family when you make use of the function known as Family Photo Stream.
- You can maintain your calendar in addition to sharing family calendars.
- Communicate whereabouts with one another so that you are always aware of the whereabouts of your family members.
- You may use Find My iPhone from any other device in the family group to locate the iPhones and iPads belonging to other members of the family.
- The **"Seek to Buy"** feature enables parents to require their children under the age of 18 to ask permission before actually

144

purchasing material from the iTunes and App Store; you may approve or reject requests remotely.

- If your child is under the age of 18, you can require them to ask permission before actually purchasing the content.

Getting started with Family Sharing on the iPhone 13 mini, including how to enable it:

The family organizer is the individual who should begin the process of setting up Family Sharing initially. You, as the organizer of the family, will be the one to receive requests to make purchases, and more importantly, you will agree to pay for any purchases made by any member of the family group, regardless of whether they are an adult or a child.

1. Launch the Settings app on the iPhone 13 mini.

2. Select the **Apple ID banner** that is located at the top of the screen.

3. From the drop-down menu, choose the option **"Set Up Family Sharing."**

4. From the drop-down menu, choose the **Get Started option**.

5. Click the button labeled Continue. It is up to you whether or not you want to submit an image in advance, although doing so is not needed.

6. Choose the **Continue option** to share your purchases with others.

7. Tap the Continue button once you have confirmed your payment method. Please take note that this is one of the things that may be changed in the settings.

8. Touch **Press the Share Your Location option** if you want to let family members know where you are, or tap the **Not Now option** if you don't want to do so.

9. From the drop-down menu, choose the option to **Add a Family Member**.

10.   Start entering someone's name and go from there.

11.   Tap the person's name who you would want to add as a Family Member, and then choose them from the drop-down menu.

12.   When prompted, enter, the security code on the credit card to verify that you are the event organizer.

Simply keep adding new members of the family until you've accounted for every member of the family (up to 6 people). They will be asked to accept your invitation through email as well as a push notification that will be sent to their phones. After they have done so, the account of the family organizer will be debited automatically for any further purchases. In addition to this, they will get instant access to the purchases made by the other members of the group.

How to accept an invitation to participate in Family Sharing using iPhone 13 mini

The steps:

1. Select **Settings** from the Home screen menu on your device.
2. Click the **Apple ID banner** that is located at the top of the screen.
3. Pick out your invitations. It should have a 1 in the space next to it.
4. Select the **Accept option** using the button.
5. Activate the button labeled **"Confirm."** *Note:* If you want to use a different Apple ID, you may do so by choosing the option that says **"Not (your name) or desires to use another ID?"**
6. To show others what you've bought, hit the **Continue button**.

7. To share your location, choose either **Share Your Location or Not Now from the drop-down menu**.

Steps involved in putting someone in a position of parental or guardian responsibility

To appoint someone as a parent or guardian of a child, you need to be the **"family organizer,"** which is equivalent to the person who established the Family Sharing group.

1. Launch the **Settings app** on the iPhone 13 mini.
2. Touch the **Apple ID banner** that is located at the top of the screen.
3. From the drop-down box, choose the option to Share with Family.

4. Choose the parent or guardian with who you would want to have legal custody of your kid.

5. Toggle the switch that is located next to Parent and Guardian (green is on).

Take note that all the children who are part of your Family Sharing group will now submit their purchase requests to that specific person. This suggests that if one parent is unable to accept a request due to a disagreement, the other parent may be able to do it instead. However, just a single person, not both of them together, will be required to approve a request.

How to Use Screen Time

To begin using Screen Time, go to **"Settings"** and then choose **"Screen Time."** The following are some instances of what you are capable of doing.

Average per Day

Throughout the day, you will be able to read a summary of your actions at the very top of the Screen Time app. You can receive a breakdown of the programs you used and the amount of time you spent using them by going to **"See All Activity."**

DownTime

You can arrange periods in Downtime when you want to force yourself to take a break from staring at the computer, and this allows you to do so. This is accomplished by limiting access to the programs that you are most likely to engage in conversation with. These limitations are not ironclad; as you will find out in the next sections, you can close Downtime anytime you see fit.

To get started, choose a time when you won't be using your phone and write it down.

- Tap on the **"Downtime"** button to turn it on and off.

- Select the days (either every day or on select days) and periods during which you do not want your favorite iPhone apps to consume too much of your time. You may do this either permanently or temporarily. During specific hours, you will be restricted to using just the programs that you have already chosen, in addition to making phone calls. During business hours, you may, for instance, deactivate Facebook and Twitter but keep the Messages app open so that you can continue to receive text messages.

- Before the start of Downtime, you will be given a heads-up on what to expect. Do not be concerned if you find that you need to continue working on an application; you will be given the choice to ask for one more minute of work time, to be reminded in 15 minutes, or to ignore the time limit for today.

Note: Please keep in mind that you can use Downtime as well as the other Screen Time capabilities on any of your iCloud-enabled devices. As a consequence of this, if you configure it on your iPhone, it will also function properly on your Mac and your iPad. To share your preferences across all of your devices, you can do so by toggling the **"Share Across Devices" option** on the main page of Page Time.

Now that you've selected when you want to take a break, one of the next things you should do is choose the programs that can continue to run in the background while you take a break.

On the main screen for Screen Time, choose the option labeled **"Always Allowed."** From this menu, you will be able to choose which apps will be available to you during any downtime that may occur.

There are two distinct groups of applications from which to select: those that are allowed and those that are Chosen.

- To pick an app to which you will always want access, even when you aren't using it, tap its name under **Choose Apps**. After doing so, the app will appear in the list of **Allowed Apps.**

- To deactivate any of the Allowed Apps, tap the minus symbol that is located next to the program, and then choose **"Remove."**

There are many different ways in which one might personalize downtime. Let's say you want to be alerted whenever particular people send you a text message. You might set up an alert. You're working on a project and you don't want to hear from any of your friends, but you do want to continue receiving messages from members of your family.

- Touch the **"Contacts"** option that is located at the very top of the **"Always Allowed"** page.

- Below the heading **"Allowed Communication,"** choose **"Specific Contacts,"** and then select the contacts that you want to be able to communicate with you at any time, even while you are offline.

It is important to note that the **"Allowed Communication"** page can also be accessed from the main Screen Time page. This is something that should be kept in mind.

How to switch the background

wallpapers

Pick a photo to serve as the wallpaper for either the Home Screen or the Lock Screen of your iPhone 13 mini. You may choose between dynamic photographs or pictures that are static.

1. Navigate to **Settings > Wallpaper > Select a New Wallpaper** to change the background image on your device.

2. Choose and carry out an activity from the list below:

- At the very top of the screen, choose an image from a selection of predefined options (Dynamic, Stills, and so on).

- When Dark Mode is activated, the wallpaper that has been tagged undergoes a visual transformation.

- Pick a photo from your collection to display (tap an album, then tap the photo).

- To zoom in on the photo you've selected, just open it up and pinch it, then use your finger to move it to a new location. To zoom out, just pinch the screen closed.

- Tap to activate **Perspective Zoom**, which, when used with certain wallpaper choices, makes your wallpaper seem to **"move"** when the viewing angle is adjusted. This option is available with specific wallpaper selections.

It is possible to disable the Perspective Zoom option by going to **Settings > Accessibility > Motion** and selecting the **Reduce Motion option**.

After selecting the Set button, choose one of the following options:

- Make sure the lock screen is active.
- Make sure you are on your Home Screen.

To activate Perspective Zoom for a wallpaper that you have already chosen, go to **Settings >**

Wallpaper, tap the image that is now shown on the Lock Screen or Home Screen, and then pick Perspective Zoom from the menu that appears.

CHAPTER FOURTEEN

How to use widgets on the Home

Screen

With the release of iOS 15 and later versions, widgets received an overhaul that freed them from the confines of the Today display and allowed them to function independently. They are now accessible on the Home screen, where they may be located among your most used apps. In addition, widgets are now offered in three different sizes: small, medium, and large. This gives users the ability to see either a tiny amount of information or all of the information they want in a single glance.

What kinds of new widgets do iOS 15 and later versions bring?

Apple is providing a few new widgets for apps that were desperately in need of one before iOS 15, but the iPhone's widgets won't be altering much due to the update. The following is an overview of the brand-new widgets that will be included in iOS 15 and later versions:

- App Store
- Contacts
- Game Center
- Mail
- Sleep

Adding a widget to your Home screen may be done via the Today view as follows:

1. Swipe to the right on the Home screen to open the Today view on your device.

2. Tap and hold the widget you want to move to the Home screen, and then choose it from the menu that appears.

3. By dragging the widget in the direction of your Home screen, you can move it there.

4. Position the widget where you would want it to appear on the Home screen.

Steps to take to add a new widget to my Home screen

1. To enter edit mode, often known as **"jiggle,"** press and hold anywhere on your Home screen. ***Note:*** This will allow you to move items about on the screen.

2. To continue, hit the **Plus button** that is located in the upper-left corner of the screen.

3. Choose a widget from the list of pre-defined options or an app whose widget

you want to use and choose it from the drop-down menu.

4. Swipe to the left or right on the widget sizes to choose a different size for the widget.

5. On the Home screen, touch and drag the widget you want to use to the position where you want it to be shown.

6. To dismiss **"jiggle mode,"** press **Done**.

Making changes to a widget

You have a broad variety of widgets to choose from, each of which may be customized to display specific information.

Detailed instructions are provided below:

1. To open a contextual menu, press and hold your finger on a widget or Smart Stack until the menu displays.

2. From the drop-down menu, choose the **Edit Widget option**. If you want to make changes to only one of the widgets in a Smart Stack, you should press the Edit button that is labeled "[Widget name]."

3. Modify the parameters of the widget so that they correspond to your specific needs. Every widget has its configuration options.

How to add a widget most efficiently to the Today view

1. From the Home screen, swipe right to get the **Today view** on your device.
2. To enter edit mode (also known as jiggle mode), touch and hold on to a blank area of the screen.
3. Tap the **Plus button** located in the upper-left corner of the screen.

4. Tap the icon of an app whose widget you want to view on the Today display, and then choose the app from the menu that appears.

5. To change the size of your widget, swipe to the left or right.

6. Choose the widget, and then use the arrow keys or the mouse to move it to the appropriate area in the Today view.

7. To quit edit mode, hit **Done**.

How to construct a Smart Stack or add a widget to an existing one

To create a Smart Stack by combining two or more widgets or to add a source of material to an existing Smart Stack, do the steps outlined in this section.

1. To add a widget to a smart stack, tap and hold the widget until it becomes highlighted.

2. Either relocate the widget to another standalone widget or construct a Smart Stack by dragging and dropping the widget onto the Smart Stack. This will build the Smart Stack.

How to make adjustments to a smart stack widget

A Smart Stack is a kind of widget that is mostly composed of additional widgets. Throughout the day, it will change the information that it displays to you to provide you access to the content that is the most relevant to you.

You can manually change a Smart Stack to fine-tune the information that is shown below:

1. While you are waiting for the context menu to appear, keep the Smart Stack widget in your hand.

2. From the drop-down menu, choose the **Edit Stack option**.

3. Tap and drag the arrangement bars to modify the order in which the material that is presented in the stack is displayed.

4. Swipe to the left in the direction of the arrow to remove a content source from the stack.

5. Select **Delete**.

6. To activate or deactivate Smart Rotate, press the switch that is located next to it.

Steps to take to remove a widget from my Home screen

1. To remove the widget from the page, select it and then press and hold the delete button until the context menu appears.

2. Choose **Remove Widget** from the list of options in the drop-down menu.

3. Make your selection from the Remove menu.

CHAPTER FIFTEEN

List of iPhone 13 mini

Troubleshooting issues

When it comes to creating a smooth and flawless experience, iPhones unquestionably stand out from the competition. However, this does not imply that Apple's most-talked-about smartphone was devoid of common problems with iPhone 13 mini. Fortunately, there are several helpful tips and strategies for repairing common iPhone 13 mini issues.

They include the following:

iPhone Cannot Link to Wi-Fi

iPhone Off or Wifi Off Wi-Fi slows down between Frequently Encountered Issues with the iPhone 13 mini and their Resolutions, as many users see. The answer is rather straightforward. You must just power down and reset the phone. Press and hold the home button and lock key simultaneously until the Apple logo appears on the screen.

After restarting the device, you shall be able to connect to Wifi. If iPhone 13 mini problems continue, go to Settings, then WiFi, then down to the bottom of the screen to reset the HTTP proxy to its default settings.

The Mobile data connection is not functioning

There are several reasons why your iPhone's mobile connection may not function. For instance, the Common Problems in iPhone 13 mini might be caused by iPhone deletion and network-related difficulties. Therefore, if you encounter this problem, ensure that there is a steady cellular connection and that there is no network outage in your region.

If the issue continues, you should reset the network settings to get rid of the sluggish network. To do so, click **General** from the Settings app on your smartphone. Now, tap the **Reset button** followed by **Reset Network Settings**. If you have successfully rejoined the network, verify that the iPhone 13 mini's Common Issues have been fixed.

iPhone is stuck on Apple Logo

The iPhone is stuck on the Apple logo, which is one of the most common problems with the iPhone 13 small that a big number of iPhone customers encounter. Fortunately, a power reset often resolves these common iPhone 13 mini issues. Therefore, if your smartphone has ever been compromised, do a hard reset.

Press the volume up button to restart an iPhone 8 or later and then press the volume-down button next. Now, tap the sidebar until the Apple logo appears on the display.

iPhone App Unpredictably Crashes or Freezes

Attempt to restart the app or your iPhone if you discover that it often freezes or stops suddenly. Verify that the program has been completely installed and updated to the most recent version from the App Store if the issue continues. Lastly, ensure that the app is compatible with iOS 15 or later on your device.

With the latest iOS, Apple has updated 32-bit applications to 64-bit ones, rendering the older ones incompatible with your device. To determine whether applications are out-of-date, go to **Settings > General > About Apps**. If all of your apps are current, you will not be able to touch Apps. If not, the arrow will lead you to a list of 32-bit applications that may be deleted.

Honestly, app stalling and crashes are the most common iPhone 13 mini issues ever seen. The good news is that it can be readily repaired. Verify that the issue program has been updated to its most recent version (**App Store > Profile**). Then, go to the app you want to update. Press the **Update button** then.

No iOS Version Update Available

One of the most frequent issues with your iPhone 13 mini is that it has not been upgraded to iOS 15 or later versions yet. The remedy is to connect your handset to a Mac or PC and force a restart, which will put your iPhone into recovery mode.

Then you will be able to see the refresh option, and when you select it, the update will begin, and your phone will function normally after it is complete. If you were unable to view the refresh option after a hard restart, try reinstating the option to delete all phone data. You will now get the most recent version of the program and will be reimbursed with a copy of your backup data.

Overheating Issues

Exposing your device to hut sun or a very hot area is likely to disable your smartphone until it cools. When you are in a position to receive a notification message, disconnect your phone's cover and accessories and keep it out of direct sunlight. Turn on Airplane Mode while your iPhone is cool to give it a rest, then disconnect it to charge while it is still hot. If overheating continues, update to iOS 15/later versions or reset all settings.

iPhone is Deactivated

The difficult aspect of forgetting your passcode is that you are forced to restore your iPhone, which erases all of your data. Likewise, so do radio tunes now and again. It! Up! The iPhone may then be restored using iTunes or recovery mode.

Face ID ceased to function

Remove any phone cover or screen protection that might impair the depth perception of the camera. Ensure that you are not wearing any facial cosmetics (sunglasses, jewelry) that might interfere with your Face ID. Remember that the iPhone only recognizes Face ID while it is in standby mode, so hold your phone upright when it is in place. If your iPhone has difficulties identifying your face, you're in danger. Reset Face ID (Settings **Face ID & Passcode Reset Face**

ID). Update to iOS 15 or later versions and do a rapid restart of your iPhone.

There are a few situations in which your iPhone requires a password instead of Face ID:

1. Switch on the iPhone or reboot the device.
2. After more than 48 hours with the iPhone unlocked.
3. After five failed Face ID unlock attempts, the iPhone is locked.
4. Following the issuance of a lengthy lock order

Defective Proximity Sensor

If you notice your ear pushing random buttons and interfering with your iPhone, the error sensor may still be active. No matter how quickly you place the device in your ear, you may find yourself playing voice notes from WhatsApp. Even if the incorrect sensor is causing Common Problems in iPhone 13 mini with the touch screen, it might be a software issue or a product feature, so don't instantly replace your screen. If you've attempted to restart, restart, or even reset the original iPhone, restore it to iTunes in DFU mode.

iPhone Data is Lost

It is frustrating to lose all of your phone's crucial data. However, this is a common issue with the iPhone 13 mini when it comes to iPhone devices. With Cloud Backup, the solution will be simple. Simply sync the device using iCloud-iPhone. Nighttime synchronization is possible while the device is locked. Your absent stuff will be accessible through iCloud. However, if you do not locate anything there, you should head to the Apple shop, where you will discover several options for recovering lost data.

Not Working/Not Opening Camera

If limits are enabled, the iPhone camera will not function. You may verify this by heading to **Settings > General > Camera**. The majority of common issues with the iPhone 13 small camera will be addressed here. If the camera continues to be inoperable, consider restarting your phone as indicated above. And if you do not get updates, there might be a hardware issue. Bring it to the nearby iPhone service facility to repair the problem.

Rapid Power Drain

The quick battery depletion or draining was one of the most prevalent issues with the iPhone 13 mini. The best option is to close unnecessary applications. If the iPhone battery issue continues, you should contact your service provider immediately.

Water Damage

Water is the worst enemy of any electronic gadget, and the same holds true for iPhone covers. If your phone gets immersed, you may attempt a variety of methods before giving up. Immediately after withdrawing the phone from the water, you should use tissue paper to remove any excess water.

Never attempt to unlock the phone immediately, since doing so causes irreversible harm. The next step is to take a cup of rice and place your iPhone 13 mini into it. Within 24 hours, the rice will absorb the leftover liquid. Also, it is possible to dismantle the phone and dry it by hand, although it needs some expertise. If the phone continues to malfunction, you may contact your local service provider.

iPhone Refuse to Charge (Battery)

Connecting the battery to the iPhone 13 mini is one of the most common issues. There are several solutions to this issue. Remove any dust or dirt from the charging hole by wiping it.

Whether the issue persists, the next step is to examine the connecting cable to see if it is compatible with other Apple devices or other USB cables, etc. You can also attempt to reboot the device manually if that does not work. If the device is not operating, attempt a factory reset. If the issue continues, please contact your local service provider.

Touchscreen malfunction

iPhones often encounter touch screen issues, such as a non-responsive display or a dark screen. The most basic and primary remedy is to reset your device. If the gadget is not functioning, charge it for one hour. The issue will likely be resolved.

If the screen is damaged and unresponsive, there may be a hardware issue. Therefore, you must visit the iPhone screen repair location. Your issue will be resolved at a reasonable cost if you contact an authorized Apple reseller.

Bluetooth problems (not opening/connecting)

By accessing the iPhone 13 mini's General Settings and resetting all choices and settings, you may simply resolve the majority of Bluetooth-related issues. This will delete all previously stored settings and resolve the issue.

Stuck Volume Button

If the volume up button is locked, you may get irritated when calls arrive at inappropriate times. There are several solutions to this issue. You might try activating the airplane mode. Therefore, every call will be sent to voicemail. Additionally, you can muffle all noises on your smartphone. Alternatively, you should open the help-access settings and activate the help mode. From there, you can now operate your device directly from the homepage.

iPhone is Sluggish or Lags

On occasion, your iPhone may be sluggish. There are several answers to this issue, so do not fret. To speed up your iPhone 13 mini, consider uninstalling any programs, outdated data, and incorrect screenshots, as well as emptying the cache and history of your web browser.

Not Able To Backup the Data

Occasionally, the iPhone will not back up to iCloud. If this is the case, verify if the iCloud storage is full. If it is full, attempt to delete some data. In-app programs use the same amount of space as the mail app. So eliminate it. If you want to store all data, consider upgrading the storage system. Before trying any of these procedures, you may check for available iOS 15.5, or iOS 16 upgrades. If not, reset network settings by resetting Wi-Fi passwords, mobile phone settings, and VPN configurations. You may do so by navigating to Settings > General > Reset Network Settings.

CONCLUSION

The iPhone 13 mini is the start of the iPhone 13 series and it is an amazing device for low-budget device users who still want to use one of the best devices with a lesser budget. The device spots several new features including an upgraded battery capacity, faster charging, the latest iOS, and performance as it spots the A15 Bionic Processor, memory, design, display, and so much more.

Some of the discussed topics in this guide include setting up your device automatically or manually, how to use features such as Apple Pay, the camera, family sharing, Siri, and a host of other functional features. If you have the iPhone 13 mini or plan to get it soon, you should get this guide and set yourself to mastering the device in the shortest possible time.

ABOUT THE AUTHOR

Perry Hoover is a researcher, tech Entrepreneur, blogger and a technology writer, who is fond of blogging, technology research and writing. His areas of interest include Web application penetration testing, web security/architecture, cryptography, programming languages and database security. He is well versed with the latest technology, programming languages, computer hardware/software, and programming tools. He is also an expert in database security and application security architecture and penetration testing. He loves to share information about new technology and has published dozens of articles on it.

He has written articles on different aspects of IT Technologies including IT security, data storage and application development for magazines and has also published and co-published several e-books, of which the latest is on Windows 11. He has also worked with different private agencies to provide solutions to IT problems.

Made in United States
Cleveland, OH
13 August 2025

19374680R00108